Christian Prayer

East and West

Edited by Alan R. Kemp

Hermitage Desktop Press

Christian
Prayer
East and West

Edited by Alan R. Kemp

© 2017 by Hermitage Desktop Press

For more information please contact the publisher:

Hermitage Desktop Press
P.O. Box 167
Vaughn, WA 98394

ISBN: 978-0692854549

Printed in the United States of America

Table of Contents

ACKNOWLEDGEMENTS

I wish to gratefully acknowledge the holy men and women who brought these prayers into being and those who use, and have used, these prayers to the benefit of their interior spiritual life.

INTRODUCTION

Many of the prayers contained within this book were originally published in *A Free Catholic Concise Liturgy: And Other Useful Writings*, which was first published by the editor of the present book in 2015. A few others, including "The Prayer of the Chalice," and the Liberal Catholic "Thee we Adore ..." were first published in our *Altar Training Manual*. They are reprinted here to make them more available to a wider audience of people wishing to deepen their interior spiritual life.

THE ASCENSION MOVEMENT–A BRANCH OF THE MYSTICAL BODY OF CHRIST

The Ascension is a spiritual, historical, event. The Ascension movement is a spiritual movement "without ceiling" or affiliation with any other established ecclesiastical body.

While the Ascension movement is born of the vision of a "Free Catholicism," a fledgling "Independent Catholic" movement, the "Emerging Church," and "Jewish Renewal," it is really a much larger stirring of Spirit that beckons persons of faith to transcend old ways that no longer work and ascend to higher levels of consciousness and spiritual living. To use a metaphor from New Testament scripture: Don't put new wine into old wineskins.

In keeping with the wisdom of spiritual reflection, we can, however, say Ascension is open to exploring new insights in conversation with and respect for ancient traditions.

If your own Spirit resonates with what you're reading, perhaps you were already part of the Ascension movement and didn't even know it. If so, read on.

CHRISTIC

We are a part the one Mystical Body of Christ. We acknowledge Jesus, the Christ, as Emanuel, God incarnated in human form, as our founder, inspiration, living head, teacher, and eternal high priest. We accept the historic creeds as divinely inspired, but we also acknowledge they were often used to exclude rather than embrace all the people of God. We uphold the great commandments of both Hebrew scripture and New Testament: love God with all you heart, mind, and strength; likewise, your fellow human beings, like yourself, all of whom were created in God's divine image.

VISION OF A FREE CATHOLICISM

We see a Free Catholicism as a movement of Spirit endeavoring to break loose from old ways that no longer work; reclaiming the original blessing of the primitive, universal, Church. We are a mystical movement without ceiling, walls, or affiliation with any other ecclesiastical body. We do, however, lay claim to apostolic succession, the tradition in which bishops trace their consecrations, from bishop to bishop, in an unbroken line back to the original apostles.

INDEPENDENT CATHOLIC MOVEMENT

Independent Catholic churches are Catholic groups not in communion with the Roman Catholic Church, who hold valid apostolic succession for their bishops, and are not formally affiliated with other historic churches. Most trace their apostolic succession through bishops of the Old Catholic and Oriental Orthodox churches. There are over 100 such groups in the United States today.

Although the term Old Catholic was first used in 1853 to describe those Catholics belonging to independent see at Utrecht in the Netherlands, most scholars date the "modern" Old Catholic movement to the 1870s, after the First Vatican Council declared the Roman Catholic Pope infallible when speaking "ex-cathedra" on matters of faith and morals. These Old Catholic churches were supported by the independent Old Catholic Archbishop of Utrecht, who ordained their priests and bishops. Later, they united more formally as the Utrecht Union of Churches.

The Oriental Orthodox churches, sometimes called "Non-Calcedonian," include the Armenian, Assyrian, Coptic, and the Syrian "Jacobite" churches, which did not ratify the declarations of the Council of Calcedon, in 451 A.D.

The Independent Catholic movement came to Great Britain in 1908 when Arnold Harris Mathew was consecrated a bishop in the Old Catholic Church, which, incorrectly believed he had a significant following in the United Kingdom, and also that there would be a wave of clergy wanting to leave the Church of England as a result of Pope Leo XIII's declaration that Anglican orders were null and void. Mathew believed that Old Catholicism would provide a home for these disaffected clergy. However, the expected mass conversions never happened. Before breaking with the Union of Utrecht, however, Mathew consecrated several persons to the episcopacy, from whom a number of new churches quickly developed, including the Liberal Catholic Church, whose first bishop was James Wedgwood, consecrated by F.S. Willoughby, who in turn had been consecrated by Mathew.

The founding bishop and leader of the Ascension organization, was consecrated by bishops of the Catholic Apostolic Church of Antioch, who trace

4

their the own apostolic succession, or lineage, through both Old Catholic and Oriental Orthodox bishops.

EMERGING CHURCH MOVEMENT

The Emerging Church Movement is a Christian movement of the late 20th and early 21st century. Participants are variously described as evangelical, post-evangelical, liberal, post-liberal, charismatic, neo-charismatic and post-charismatic. Participants seek a faith that will help them live authentic lives in what they believe to be a troubled "postmodern" world. Proponents often call the movement a "conversation" to emphasize its developing and decentralized nature, its vast range of standpoints, and its commitment to dialogue.

EMBRACING JEWISH RENEWAL

We embrace the oldest of Christian traditions, acknowledging that Jesus, the Christ, was a Jew. Not only this, but a pious Jew, steeped in his faith and culture, including its mystical traditions, like a child raised on mother's milk. The terms Jewish Renewal and Jewish Reconstruction describe the teachings and practices of present-day Jews that are attempting to reinvigorate Judaism with mystical, musical, and meditative practices. It often includes Judaism's prophetic and mystical traditions. It brings kabbalistic and Hasidic theory and practice into a non-Orthodox, egalitarian framework, a phenomenon sometimes referred to as neo-Hasidism. Like Hasidic Jews, Renewal and Reconstruction Jews often add ecstatic practices to traditional worship, such as meditation, chant and dance. In augmenting traditional ritual, adherents also borrow freely and openly from the mystical traditions of other faiths, e.g. Buddhism and Sufism. The movement's most prominent leader was Rabbi Zalman Schachter-Shalomi.

SACRAMENTAL

We are sacramental. We hold that the sacraments are both visible signs, or a manifestations, of divine grace, and expressions of divine power that are made available to help us in life and in our spiritual growth. We make the sacraments of Holy Eucharist (Communion), Reconciliation (Penance), Holy Unction (healing of the sick), and Holy Matrimony available to all who seek them. Baptism is freely conferred as a rite of formal initiation into Christ's mystical body. Confirmation seals the commitment to a Christian way of life. Ordination to Holy Orders is an initiation available to qualified candidates called to serve God and God's people.

CONTEMPORARY

We maintain that eternal truth cloaks itself in garb appropriate to the age, and that the outward expressions of religion should keep pace with human development. We do not shrink from new knowledge. Our form of Free Catholicism embraces ancient truth, sacred scripture, purposeful prayer, traditional liturgy, but strives to creatively explore new expressions of ritual, art, community-building, and healing.

FELLOWSHIP

Our church is a spiritual fellowship of sojourners on the spiritual path. We give ourselves, and others, encouragement to live revealed truth. To live the truth is to become ever more the Christ, the true Self, the source of real happiness and abiding fellowship.

LOVE CENTERED

We are part of a movement of love. We accept Saint John's testimony that God is Love. For us, Christ's ministry is the law of love: "Love the Lord, thy God, with thy whole heart, thy whole mind and thy whole strength; and love thy neighbor as thyself. This is the whole of the Law and the prophets." Saint Augustine epitomized Christian ethics in the precept, "Love and do as you will."

UNIVERSAL

We maintain that the Holy Spirit acts through pure channels everywhere, regardless of age, sex, race, creed or culture. There is only one true God, however this God is known or worshipped; hence, there is eternally only one holy universal Presence, regardless of the cultural form it happens to assume in a given time and place. We revere the saints, sages, and holy ones of all ages and places.

MYSTICAL

We are a mystical movement, keeping in mind the Old Testament words, "Be still and know I AM" - God. We honor a saying attributed to Christ, "The kingdom of heaven lies within you and outside you," and acknowledge that the great advancements in acquiring spiritual truth are made by those who learn to look within. If God is Love, then it is through our love that we come to a real and abiding knowledge of God. For Christians, love is spiritual knowledge par excellence.

SPIRITUAL

We seek to draw back the veil, first to discover the deeper intellectual import and then the experiential dimension which is the true meaning of spiritual symbolism in scripture, ritual, liturgy and theology.

OPEN COMMUNION

We hold that a purpose of Christian Fellowship is to perpetuate the historical sacramental tradition as instituted by Jesus Christ. We maintain that the sacraments are channels of divine grace. Therefore, we make them easily available to all. Since the Eucharist puts us in communion with the Christ, it is a channel of Grace without parallel. Therefore, at our altars all reverent persons are welcome to receive communion.

OPEN HOLY ORDERS

Holy Orders are open to all qualified candidates. While we value the principle of the "priesthood of the laity," we also we recognize the importance of valid Holy Orders and professional preparation of clergy. Our solution is to make orders available to all qualified candidates who are called and chosen. Other than demonstrating educational aptitude and prior life experience that shows academic and spiritual evidence of the potential to successfully complete a program of priestly formation at the graduate level, there are no other restrictions.

We have developed a highly decentralized program of study that offers structured guidance and mentorship for those willing to undergo rigorous study and practice that may lead to ordination as a "barefoot priest" within the context of Free Catholic Renewal. We welcome students from diverse backgrounds and spiritual traditions. The Program may either supplement other studies or serve as the primary preparation for ordained ministry. Each candidate's formation process is supervised by a Formation Committee, including a Formation Director selected by the Program, the candidate, and at least one other mentor selected by the candidate, usually a clergy member, educator, spiritual director, counselor, or other individual poised to support and help the candidate. Those who achieve ordination must be prepared to support themselves as "barefoot priests" in the world. We are not able to provide financial support.

AN ANTHOLOGY OF COMMON PRAYERS

INTRODUCTION TO THE JESUS PRAYER

by H.R.H. Princess Ileana of Romania

Reprinted with permission of Forward Movement Publications, 412 Sycamore St. Cincinnati, Ohio.

Lord Jesus Christ, Son of God, have mercy upon me, a sinner.

I have often read the Jesus Prayer in prayer books and heard it in church, but my attention was drawn to it first some years ago in Romania. There in the small Monastery of Smbata, tucked away at the foot of the Carpathians in the heart of the deep forest, its little white church reflected in a crystal clear mountain pond, I met a monk who practiced the "prayer of the heart". Profound peace and silence reigned at Smbata in those days; it was a place of rest and strength.-I pray God it still is.

I have wandered far since I last saw Smbata, and all the while the Jesus Prayer lay as a precious gift buried in my heart. It remained inactive until a few years ago, when I read *The Way of a Pilgrim.** Since then I have been seeking to practice it continually. At times I lapse; nonetheless, the prayer has opened unbelievable vistas within my heart and soul.

The Jesus Prayer, or the Prayer of the Heart, centers on the Holy Name itself. It may be said in its entirety: "Lord Jesus Christ, Son of God, have mercy upon me, a sinner"; it may be changed to "us sinners" or to other persons named, or it may be shortened.

The power lies in the name of Jesus; thus "Jesus" alone, may fulfill the whole need of the one who prays.

The Prayer goes back to the New Testament and has had a long, traditional use. The method of contemplation based upon the Holy Name is attributed to St. Simeon, called the New Theologian (949-1022). When he was 14 years old, St. Simeon had a vision of heavenly light in which he seemed to be separated from his body. Amazed, and overcome with an overpowering joy, he felt a consuming humility, and cried, borrowing the Publican's prayer (Luke 18:13), "Lord Jesus, have mercy upon me." Long after the vision had disappeared, the great joy returned to St. Simeon each time he repeated the prayer; and he taught his disciples to worship likewise. The prayer evolved into its expanded form: "Lord Jesus Christ, Son of God, have mercy upon me, a sinner." In this guise it has come down to us frown generation to generation of pious monks and laymen.

The invocation of the Holy Name is not peculiar to the Orthodox Church but is used by Roman Catholics, Anglicans, and Protestants, though to a lesser degree. On Mount Sinai and Athos the monks worked out a whole system of contemplation based upon this simple prayer, practiced in complete silence. These monks came to be known as Quietists (in Greek: "Hesychasts").

St. Gregory Palamas (1296-1359), the last of the great Church Fathers, became the exponent of the Hesychasts. He won, after a long drawn out battle, an irrefutable place for the Jesus Prayer and the Quietists within the Church. In the 18th century when tsardom hampered monasticism in Russia, and the Turks crushed Orthodoxy in Greece, the Neamtzu monastery in Moldavia (Romania) became one of the great centers for the Jesus Prayer.

The Prayer is held to be so outstandingly spiritual because it is focused wholly on Jesus: all thoughts, striving, hope, faith and love are outpoured in devotion to God the Son. It fulfills two basic injunctions of the New Testament. In one, Jesus said: I say unto you, Whatsoever ye shall ask the Father; in my name, he will give it you. Hitherto have ye asked nothing in my name: ask, and ye shall receive, that your joy may be full." (John 16:23, 24). In the other precept we find St. Paul's injunction to pray without ceasing,

(I. Thess. 5:17). Further, it follows Jesus' instructions upon how to pray (which He gave at the same time He taught His followers the Lord's Prayer). When thou prayest, enter into thy closet, and when thou hast shut thy door, pray to thy Father which is in secret; and thy Father which seeth in secret shall reward thee openly. (Math 6:6).

And Jesus taught that all impetus, good and bad, originates in men's hearts. "A good man out of the good treasure of his heart bringeth forth that which is good; and an evil man out of the evil treasure of his heart bringeth forth that which is evil: for of the abundance of the heart his mouth speaketh" (Luke 6:45).

Upon these and many other precepts of the New Testament as well as the Old, the Holy Fathers, even before St. Simeon, based their fervent and simple prayer. They developed a method of contemplation in

12

which unceasing prayer became as natural as breathing, following the rhythmic cadence of the heart beat.

All roads that lead to God are beset with pitfalls because the enemy (Satan) ever lies in wait to trip us up. He naturally attacks most assiduously when we are bent on finding our way to salvation, for that is what he most strives to hinder. In mystical prayer the temptations we encounter exceed all others in danger; because our thoughts are on a higher level, the allurements are proportionally subtler. Someone said that "mysticism started in mist and ended in schism"; this cynical remark, spoken by an unbeliever, has a certain truth in it. Mysticism is of real spiritual value only when it is practiced with absolute sobriety.

At one time a controversy arose concerning certain Quietists who fell into excessive acts of piety and fasting because they lost the sense of moderation upon which our Church lays so great a value. We need not dwell upon misuses of the Jesus Prayer, except to realize that all exaggerations are harmful and that we should at all times use self-restraint. "Practice of the Jesus Prayer is the traditional fulfillment of the injunction of the Apostle Paul to 'pray always:' it has nothing to do with the mysticism which is the heritage of pagan ancestry."*

The Orthodox Church is full of deep mystic life which she guards and encompasses with the strength of her traditional rules; thus her mystics seldom go astray. "The 'ascetical life' is a life in which 'acquired' virtues, i.e., virtues resulting from a personal effort, only accompanied by that general grace which God grants to every good will, prevail. The 'mystical life' is a life in which the gifts of the Holy Spirit are predominant over human efforts, and in which 'infused' virtues are predominant over the 'acquired' ones; the soul has become more passive than active. Let us use a classical comparison. Between the ascetic life, that is, the life in which human action predominates, and the mystical life, that is, the life in which God's action predominates, there is the same difference as between rowing a boat and sailing it; the oar is the ascetic effort, the sail is the mystical passivity which is unfurled to catch the divine wind"* The Jesus Prayer is the core of mystical prayer, and it can be used by anyone, at any time. There is nothing mysterious about this (let us not confuse "mysterious" with "mystic"). We start by following the precepts and examples frequently given by our Lord. First, go aside into a quiet place: Come ye yourselves apart into a desert place, and rest awhile" (Mark 6:31); "Study to be quiet" (I. Thess. 4:11); then pray in secret--alone and in silence.

The phrases "to pray in secret alone and in silence" need, I feel, a little expanding. "Secret" should be understood as it is used in the Bible: for instance, Jesus tells us to do our charity secretly--not letting the left hand know what the right one does. We should not parade our devotions, nor boast about them. "Alone" means to separate ourselves from our immediate surroundings and disturbing influences. As a matter of fact, never are we in so much company as when we pray " . . . seeing we also are compassed about with so great a cloud of witnesses . . ." (Hebrews 12:1). The witnesses are all those who pray: Angels, Archangels, saints and sinners, the living and the dead. It is in prayer, especially the Jesus Prayer, that we become keenly aware of

14

belonging to the living body of Christ. In "silence" implies that we do not speak our prayer audibly. We do not even meditate on the words; we use them only to reach beyond them to the essence itself.

In our busy lives this is not easy, yet it can be done--we can each of us find a few minutes in which to use a prayer consisting of only a few words, or even only one. This prayer should be repeated quietly, unhurriedly, thoughtfully. Each thought should be concentrated on Jesus, forgetting all else, both joys and sorrows. Any stray thought, however good or pious, can become an obstacle. When you embrace a dear one you do not stop to meditate how and why you love--you just love wholeheartedly. It is the same when spiritually we grasp Jesus the Christ to our heart. If we pay heed to the depth and quality of our love, it means that we are preoccupied with our own reactions, rather than giving ourselves unreservedly to Jesus--holding nothing back. *Think* the prayer as you breathe in and out; calm both mind and body, using as rhythm the heartbeat. Do not search for words, but go on repeating the Prayer, or Jesus' name alone, in love and adoration. That is ALL! Strange--in this little there is more than all!

It is good to have regular hours for prayer and to retire whenever possible to the same room or place, possibly before an icon. The icon is loaded with the objective presence of the One depicted, and thus greatly assists our invocation. Orthodox monks and nuns find that to use a rosary (prayer rope) helps to keep the attention fixed. Or you may find it best quietly to close your eyes--focusing them inward.

The Jesus Prayer can be used for worship and

petition; as intercession, invocation, adoration, and as thanksgiving. It is a means by which we lay all that is in our hearts, both for God and man, at the feet of Jesus. It is a means of communion with God and with all those who pray. The fact that we can train our hearts to go on praying even when we sleep, keeps us uninterruptedly within the community of prayer. This is no fanciful statement; many have experienced this life-giving fact. We cannot, of course, attain this continuity of prayer all at once, but it is achievable; for all that is worthwhile we must ". . . run with patience the race that is set before us . . ." (Hebrews 12:1).

I had a most striking proof of uninterrupted communion with all those who pray when I lately underwent surgery. I lay long under anesthesia. "Jesus" had been my last conscious thought, and the first word on my lips as I awoke. It was marvelous beyond words to find that although I knew nothing of what was happening to my body I never lost cognizance of being prayed-for and of praying myself. After such an experience one no longer wonders that there are great souls who devote their lives exclusively to prayer.

Prayer has always been of very real importance to me, and the habit formed in early childhood of morning and evening prayer has never left me; but in the practice of the Jesus Prayer I am but a beginner. I would, nonetheless, like to awaken interest in this prayer because, even if I have only touched the hem of a heavenly garment, I have touched it--and the joy is so great I would share it with others. It is not every man's way of prayer; you may not find in it the same joy that I find, for your way may be quite a different one--yet equally bountiful.

In fear and joy, in loneliness and companionship, it is ever with me. Not only in the silence of daily devotions, but at all times and in all places. It transforms, for me, frowns into smiles; it beautifies, as if a film had been washed off an old picture so that the colors appear clear and bright, like nature on a warm spring day after a shower. Even despair has become attenuated and repentance has achieved its purpose.

When I arise in the morning, it starts me joyfully upon a new day. When I travel by air, land, or sea, it sings within my breast When I stand upon a platform and face my listeners, it beats encouragement. When I gather my children around me, it murmurs a blessing. And at the end of a weary day, when I lay me down to rest, I give my heart over to Jesus: "(Lord) into thy hands I commend my spirit". I sleep--but my heart as it beats prays on: "JESUS."

ACT OF FAITH

O my God, I firmly believe that you are one God in three divine Persons, Father, Son, and Holy Spirit; I believe that your divine Son became man and died for our sins, and that he will come to judge the living and the dead. I believe these and all the truths which the Holy Catholic Church teaches, because you revealed them, who can neither deceive nor be deceived.

ACT OF HOPE

O my God, relying on your infinite goodness and promises, I hope to obtain pardon of my sins, the help of your grace, and life everlasting, through the merits of Jesus Christ, my Lord and Redeemer.

ACT OF LOVE

O my God, I love you above all things, with my whole heart and soul, because you are all good and worthy of all my love. I love my neighbor as myself for the love of you. I forgive all who have injured me and I ask pardon of all whom I have injured.

GLORY BE...

Glory be to the Father, and to the Son, and to the Holy Spirit ... As it was in the beginning, is now, and will be for ever. AMEN.

OUR FATHER

Our Father, who art in heaven, hallowed be thy name; thy kingdom come thy will be done, on earth as it is in heaven.

Give us this day our daily bread, and forgive us our trespasses as we forgive those who trespass against us, and lead us not into temptation, but deliver us from evil.

(For the kingdom, the power, and the glory are yours, now and for ever.)
AMEN.

HAIL MARY

Hail Mary, full of grace. The Lord is with Thee. Blessed art thou among women, and blessed is the fruit of thy womb, Jesus. Holy Mary, Mother of God, pray for us sinners, now and at the hour of our death. AMEN.

O MY JESUS

O my Jesus, forgive us our sins, save us from the fires of hell, lead all souls to Heaven, especially those who have the most need of your mercy. AMEN.

MORNING PRAYER

In the name of our Lord Jesus Christ I will begin this day. I thank you, Lord, for having preserved me during the night. I will do my best to make all I do today pleasing to You and in accordance with Your will. My dear mother Mary, watch over me this day. My Guardian Angel, take care of me. St. Joseph and all you saints of God, pray for me... (followed by

Daily Offering)

DAILY OFFERING

O Jesus, through the immaculate heart of Mary, I offer you my prayers, works, joys and sufferings of this day in union with the holy sacrifice of the Mass throughout the world. I offer them for all the intentions of your sacred heart: the salvation of souls, reparation for sin, the reunion of all Christians. I offer them for the intentions of our bishops and of all the apostles of prayer.

EVENING PRAYER

O my God, at the end of this day I thank You most heartily for all the graces I have received from You. I am sorry that I have not made a better use of them. I am sorry for all the sins I have committed against You. Forgive me, O my God, and graciously protect me this night. Blessed Virgin Mary, my dear heavenly mother, take me under your protection. St. Joseph, my dear Guardian Angel, and all you saints of God, pray for me. Sweet Jesus, have pity on all poor sinners, and save them from hell. Have mercy on the suffering souls in purgatory... (followed by an Act of Contrition)

ACT OF CONTRITION

O my God, I am heartily sorry for having offended You and I detest all my sins, because I dread the loss of heaven and the pains of hell, but most of all because they offend you, my God, who are all good and deserving of all my love. I firmly resolve, with the help of your grace, to confess my sins, to do penance and to amend my life.

PRAYER BEFORE MEALS

Bless us Oh Lord, and these thy gifts, which we are about to receive, from thy bounty, through Christ, Our Lord. AMEN.

ANIMA CHRISTI

Soul of Christ, make me holy. Body of Christ, save me. Blood of Christ, fill me with love. Water from Christ's side, wash me. Passion of Christ, strengthen me. Good Jesus, hear me. Within your wounds, hide me. Never let me be parted from you. From the evil enemy, protect me. At the hour of my death, call me. And tell me to come to you. That with your saints I may praise you. Through all eternity. AMEN.

GUARDIAN ANGEL PRAYER (OLD)

O Holy Angel, attendant of my wretched soul and of mine afflicted life, forsake me not, a sinner, neither depart from me for mine inconstancy. Give no place to the evil demon to subdue me with the oppression of this mortal body; but take me by my wretched and outstretched hand, and lead me in the way of salvation. Yea, O holy Angel of God, the guardian and protector of my hapless soul and body, forgive me all things whatsoever wherewith I have troubled thee, all the days of my life, and if I have sinned in anything this day. Shelter me in this present night, and keep me from every affront of the enemy, lest I anger God by any sin; and intercede with the Lord in my behalf, that He might strengthen me in the fear of Him, and make me a worthy servant of His goodness. AMEN.

PRAYER TO OUR LADY

Remember, O most loving Virgin Mary, that never was it known that anyone who fled to your protection, implored your help, or sought your intercession was left unaided. Inspired with this confidence, we turn to you, O Virgins of virgins, our Mother. To you we come, before you we stand, sinful and sorrowful. O Mother of the Word Incarnate, do not despise our petitions, but in your mercy hear us and answer us. AMEN.

PRAYER TO THE HOLY SPIRIT

Breathe into me Holy Spirit, That all my thoughts may be holy. Move in me, Holy Spirit, that my work, too, may be holy. Attract my heart, Holy Spirit, that I may love only what is holy. Strengthen me, Holy Spirit, that I may defend all that is holy. Protect me, Holy Spirit, that I always may be holy. AMEN.

ANOTHER PRAYER TO THE HOLY SPIRIT

Spirit of wisdom and understanding, enlighten our minds to perceive the mysteries of the universe in relation to eternity. Spirit of right judgment and courage, guide us and make us firm in our baptismal decision to follow Jesus' way of love. Spirit of

22

knowledge and reverence, help us to see the lasting value of justice and mercy in our everyday dealings with one another. May we respect life as we work to solve problems of family and nation, economy and ecology. Spirit of God, spark our faith, hope and love into new action each day. Fill our lives with wonder and awe in your presence which penetrates all creation. AMEN.

SAINT PATRICK'S BREASTPLATE

I bind unto myself today the strong Name of the Trinity, by invocation of the same, the Three in One and One in three.

I bind this day to me for ever, by power of faith, Christ's incarnation; His baptism in the Jordan River; His death on cross for my salvation; His bursting from the spiced tomb; His riding up the heavenly way; His coming on the day of doom; I bind unto myself today.

I bind unto myself the power of the great love of the Cherubim; the sweet "Well done" in judgment hour; the service of the Seraphim, Confessors' faith, Apostles' word, the Patriarchs' prayers, the Prophets' scrolls; all good deeds done unto the Lord, and purity of simple souls.

I bind unto myself today the virtues of the starlit heaven, the glorious sun's life-giving ray, the whiteness of the moon at even, the flashing of the lightning free, the whirling wind's tempestuous shocks, the stable earth, the deep salt sea, around the old eternal rocks.

I bind unto myself today the power of God to hold

and lead, his eye to watch, his might to stay, his ear to hearken to my need. The wisdom of my God to teach, his hand to guide, his shield to ward; the Word of God to give me speech, his heavenly host to be my guard.

Against the demon snares of sin, the vice that gives temptation force, the natural lusts that war with me, the hostile ones that mar my course; or few or many, far or nigh, in every place, and in all hours, against their fierce hostility, I bind to me these holy powers.

Against all Satan's spells and wiles, against false words of heresy, against the knowledge that defiles, against the heart's idolatry, against the wizard's evil craft, against the death wound and the burning, the choking wave and poisoned shaft, protect me Christ, till your returning.

Christ be with me, Christ within me, Christ behind me, Christ before me, Christ beside me, Christ to win me, Christ to comfort and restore me, Christ beneath me, Christ above me, Christ in quiet, Christ in danger, Christ in hearts of all that love me, Christ in mouth of friend and stranger.

I bind unto myself the Name, the strong Name of the Trinity; by invocation of the same: The Three in One, and One in Three, of whom all nature has creation: Eternal Father, Spirit, Word, praise to the Lord of my salvation, salvation is of Christ the Lord.
AMEN.

PRAYER OF PEACE OF ST. FRANCIS OF ASSISI

Lord make me an instrument of your peace. Where there is hatred, let me sow love. Where there is injury, pardon. Where there is doubt, faith. Where there is despair, hope. Where there is darkness, light. And where there is sadness, joy.

O, Divine Master, grant that I may not so much seek to be consoled as to console, to be understood, as to understand, to be loved, as to love; For it is in giving that we receive, it is in pardoning that we are pardoned, and it is in dying that we are born to eternal life.

ANYWAY BY MOTHER TERESA OF CALCUTTA

People are unreasonable, illogical, and self-centered … Love them anyway. If you do good, people will accuse you of ulterior motives … Do good anyway. If you are successful, you win false friends and true enemies … Succeed anyway. The good you do today will be forgotten tomorrow … Do good anyway. Honesty and frankness make you vulnerable. … Be honest and frank anyway. People favor underdogs but follow only top dogs … Fight for some underdogs anyway. What you spend years building may be destroyed overnight … Build anyway. People really need help but may attack you if you help them … Help people anyway. Give the world the best you have, and you'll get kicked in the teeth … Give the world the best you've got anyway.

The Fifteen Promises of Mary to Christians Who Recite the Rosary Given to St. Dominic and Blessed Alan.

1. Whoever shall faithfully serve me by the recitation of the rosary, shall receive signal graces.

2. I promise my special protection and the greatest graces to all those who shall recite the rosary.

3. The rosary shall be a powerful armor against hell, it will destroy vice, decrease sin, and defeat heresies.

4. It will cause virtue and good works to flourish; it will obtain for souls the abundant mercy of God; it will withdraw the hearts of men from the love of the world and its vanities, and will lift them to the desire of eternal things. Oh, that souls would sanctify themselves by this means.

5. The soul which recommends itself to me by the recitation of the rosary, shall not perish.

6. Whoever shall recite the rosary devoutly, applying himself to the consideration of its sacred mysteries shall never be conquered by misfortune. God will not chastise him in His justice, he shall not perish by an unprovided death; if he be just he shall remain in the grace of God, and become worthy of eternal life.

7. Whoever shall have a true devotion for the rosary shall not die without the sacraments of the Church.

8. Those who are faithful to recite the rosary shall have during their life and at their death the light of God and the plenitude of His graces; at the moment of death they shall participate in the merits of the saints in paradise.

9. I shall deliver from purgatory those who have been devoted to the rosary.

10. The faithful children of the rosary shall merit a high degree of glory in heaven.

11. You shall obtain all you ask of me by the recitation of the rosary.

12. All those who propagate the holy rosary shall be aided by me in their necessities.

13. I have obtained from my Divine Son that all the advocates of the rosary shall have for intercessors the entire celestial court during their life and at the hour of death.

14. All who recite the rosary are my sons, and brothers of my only son Jesus Christ.

15. Devotion of my rosary is a great sign of predestination.

Prayer of the Rosary

† Sign of the Cross. In the name of the Father, and of the Son, and of the Holy Spirit. AMEN.

In the western tradition, said while making the sign of the Cross by moving the right hand from the forehead to the chest, to the left shoulder, then to the right shoulder. In the eastern tradition this is done with the first two fingers and thumb together, from right to left.

The Apostles' Creed

- Our Father

- Hail Mary
- Hail Mary
- Hail Mary

• Meditation on first mystery

◊ (Medal)

Our Father

- Hail Mary
- Hail Mary
- Hail Mary
- Hail Mary
- Hail Mary
- Hail Mary
- Hail Mary
- Hail Mary
- Hail Mary
- Hail Mary

Glory be
Oh my Jesus

• Meditation on second mystery

Our Father

- Hail Mary
- Hail Mary
- Hail Mary
- Hail Mary
- Hail Mary
- Hail Mary
- Hail Mary
- Hail Mary
- Hail Mary
- Hail Mary

Glory be
Oh my Jesus

• Meditation on third mystery

Our Father

- Hail Mary
- Hail Mary
- Hail Mary
- Hail Mary
- Hail Mary
- Hail Mary
- Hail Mary
- Hail Mary
- Hail Mary
- Hail Mary

Glory be
Oh my Jesus

- Meditation on fourth mystery

Our Father

- Hail Mary
- Hail Mary
- Hail Mary
- Hail Mary
- Hail Mary
- Hail Mary
- Hail Mary
- Hail Mary
- Hail Mary
- Hail Mary

Glory be
Oh my Jesus

- Meditation on fifth mystery

Our Father

- Hail Mary
- Hail Mary
- Hail Mary
- Hail Mary
- Hail Mary
- Hail Mary
- Hail Mary
- Hail Mary
- Hail Mary
- Hail Mary

Glory be
Oh my Jesus

◊ Concluding prayers: Hail, Holy Queen

The Prayers Said with the Rosary

The Apostles' Creed

I believe in God, the Father almighty, creator of heaven and earth.

I believe in Jesus Christ, his only Son, our Lord. He was conceived by the power of the Holy Spirit and born of the Virgin Mary. He suffered under Pontius Pilate, was crucified, died, and was buried. He descended to the dead. On the third day he rose again. He ascended into heaven, and is seated at the right hand of the Father. He will come again to judge the living and the dead.

I believe in the Holy Spirit, the holy catholic Church, the communion of saints, the forgiveness of sins, the resurrection of the body, and the life everlasting.

AMEN.

Our Father

Our Father, who art in heaven, hallowed be thy name thy kingdom come thy will be done on earth as it is in heaven.

Give us this day our daily bread and forgive us our trespasses as we forgive those who trespass against us and lead us not into temptation, but deliver us from evil.

(For the kingdom, the power, and the glory are yours, now and for ever.)

AMEN.

Hail Mary

Hail Mary, full of grace. The Lord is with Thee. Blessed art thou among women, and blessed is the fruit of thy womb, Jesus.

Holy Mary, Mother of God, pray for us sinners, now and at the hour of our death.

AMEN.

Glory be (Prayer of Praise)

Glory be to the Father, and to the Son, and to the Holy Spirit

As it was in the beginning, is now, and will be for ever.

AMEN.

O My Jesus (Requested by the Blessed Virgin Mary at Fatima)

O my Jesus, forgive us our sins, save us from the fires of hell, lead all souls to Heaven, especially those who have the most need of your mercy.

AMEN.

Hail, Holy Queen

Hail, holy queen, mother of mercy, our life, our sweetness, and our hope.

To you we cry, poor banished children of Eve; to you we send up our sighs, mourning and weeping in this valley of tears. Turn then, O most gracious advocate, your eyes of mercy toward us, and after this our exile, show unto us the blessed fruit of your womb, Jesus. O clement, O loving, O sweet virgin Mary.

Pray for us, O holy Mother of God.

Response:

That we may be made worthy of the promises of Christ, Let us pray; O God, whose only begotten Son, by his life, death, and resurrection, has purchased for us the rewards of eternal life, grant, we beseech you, that meditating upon these mysteries of the most holy rosary of the Blessed Virgin Mary, we may imitate what they contain and obtain what they promise.

Through the same, Christ our Lord.

AMEN.

- The Joyful Mysteries are usually said on Mondays.

- The Sorrowful Mysteries are usually said on Tuesdays and Fridays.

- The Glorious Mysteries are usually said on Wednesdays and Saturdays.

- The Luminous Mysteries are usually said on Wednesdays and Saturdays.

- The Mystery for Sunday varies with the seasons of the liturgical year. The Joyful Mysteries are on Sundays during the seasons of Advent, Christmas, and the first period of Ordinary time.

- Ash Wednesday marks the end of the first period of Ordinary time and the beginning of the season of Lent. During the season of Lent, the Sorrowful Mysteries are said on Sundays.

- The Easter season, which starts Easter Sunday, is the next season of the liturgical year. During the Easter season, and the second period of Ordinary time, which starts on Pentecost Sunday, the Glorious Mysteries are said on Sundays. The second period of Ordinary time ends with the first Sunday of Advent, when the Joyful Mysteries are said again.

The Joyful Mysteries

1.   The Annunciation to Mary: The Messenger of God Announces to Mary that she is to be the Mother of God.

Theme: Humility.

Then the angel said to her, "Do not be afraid, Mary, for you have found favor with God. Behold, you will conceive in your womb and bear a son, and you shall name him Jesus. He will be great and will be called Son of the Most High, and the Lord God will give him the throne of David his father, and he will rule over the house of Jacob forever, and of his kingdom there will be no end." Luke 1:30-33

2.   The Visitation of Mary: Mary visits and helps her cousin Elizabeth.

Theme: Love of Neighbor.

When Elizabeth heard Mary's greeting, the infant leaped in her womb, and Elizabeth, filled with the holy Spirit, cried out in a loud voice and said, "Most blessed are you among women, and blessed is the fruit of your womb." Luke 1:41-42

3.   The Nativity of Our Lord: Mary gives birth to Jesus in a stable in Bethlehem.

Theme: Spirit of Poverty.

The angel said to them, "Do not be afraid; for behold, I proclaim to you good news of great joy that will be for all people. For today, in the city of David a savior

has been born for you who is Messiah and Lord"
Luke 2:10-11

4.   The Presentation of the Child Jesus in the Temple: Jesus is presented in the Temple.

Theme: Obedience to God's Will

"Now, Master, you may let your servant go in peace, according to your word, for my eyes have seen your salvation, which you prepared in sight of all the peoples, a light for revelation to the Gentiles, and glory for your people Israel." Luke 2:29-32

5.   The Finding of Our Lord in the Temple.

Theme: Fidelity to Vocation, Joy in finding Jesus.

When his parents saw him, they were astonished, and his mother said to him, "Son, why have you done this to us? Your father and I have been looking for you with great anxiety." And he said to them, "Why were you looking for me? Did you not know that I must be in my Father's house?" But they did not understand what he said to them. He went down with them and came to Nazareth, and was obedient to them; and his mother kept all these things in her heart. And Jesus advanced [in] wisdom and age and favor before God and man. Luke 2:48-52

The Sorrowful Mysteries

1.   The Agony in the Garden: Jesus undergoes his agony in the Garden of Gethsemane.

Theme: Spirit of Prayer, Sorrow for Sin

Then he said to them, "My soul is sorrowful even to death. Remain here and keep watch with me." He advanced a little and fell prostrate in prayer, saying, "My Father, if it is possible, let this cup pass from me; yet, not as I will, but as you will." Matthew 26:38-39

2.   The Scourging at the Pillar: Jesus is scourged at the pillar.

Theme: Modesty and Purity

Then Pilate took Jesus and had him scourged. John 19:1

3.   The Crowning with Thorns: Jesus is crowned with thorns.

Theme: Courage

The soldiers led him away inside the palace, that is, the praetorium, and assembled the whole cohort. They clothed him in purple and, weaving a crown of thorns, placed it on him. Mark 15:16-17

4.   The Carrying of the Cross: Jesus carries the cross to Calvary.

Theme: Patience in Suffering

[A]nd carrying the cross himself he went out to what is called the Place of the Skull, in Hebrew, Golgotha. John 19:18

5.   The Crucifixion and Death of Our Lord on the Cross: Jesus dies on the cross for our sins.

Theme: Self-denial, Perseverance

After this, aware that everything was now finished, in order that the scripture might be fulfilled, Jesus said, "I thirst." There was a vessel filled with common wine. So they put a sponge soaked in wine on a sprig of hyssop and put it up to his mouth. When Jesus had taken the wine, he said, "It is finished." And bowing his head, he handed over the spirit. John 19:28-30

The Glorious Mysteries

1.   The Resurrection of Our Lord: Jesus rises from the dead.

Theme: Faith

He said to them, "Do not be amazed! You seek Jesus of Nazareth, the crucified. He has been raised; he is not here. Behold, the place where they laid him. But go and tell his disciples and Peter, 'He is going before you to Galilee; there you will see him, as he told you.'" Mark 16:6-8

2.   The Ascension of Our Lord: Jesus ascends into heaven. Hope

While they were looking intently at the sky as he was going, suddenly two men dressed in white garments stood beside them. They said, "Men of Galilee, why are you standing there looking at the sky? This Jesus who has been taken up from you into heaven will return in the same way as you have seen him going into heaven." Acts 1:10-11

3.   The Descent of the Holy Spirit upon the Apostles: The Holy Spirit comes to the apostles and the Blessed Mother.

Theme: Wisdom, Love of God, Zeal, Fortitude

When the time for Pentecost was fulfilled, they were all in one place together. And suddenly there came from the sky a noise like a strong driving wind, and it filled the entire house in which they were. Then there appeared to them tongues as of fire, which parted and came to rest on each one of them. Acts 2:1-4

4.   The Assumption of the Blessed Virgin Mary into Heaven: The Mother of Jesus is taken into heaven.

Theme: Eternal Happiness, Grace of a

Happy Death

As an apple tree among the trees of the woods, so is my lover among men. I delight to rest in his shadow, and his fruit is sweet to my mouth. He brings me into the banquet hall and his emblem over me is love. Strengthen me with raisin cakes, refresh me with apples, for I am faint with love. His left hand is under my head and his right arm embraces me. Song of Songs 2:3-6

5.   The Coronation of Our Lady as Queen of Heaven and Earth: Mary is crowned queen of heaven and earth.

Theme: Devotion to Mary and Final Perseverance, Trust in Mary's Intercession

And Mary said, "My soul proclaims the greatness of the Lord; my spirit rejoices in God my savior. For he has looked upon his handmaid's lowliness; behold, from now on will all ages call me blessed." Luke 1:46-4

The Luminous Mysteries

1.   The Baptism of Our Lord in the Jordan

Lesson: Openness to the Holy Spirit

Then Jesus came from Galilee to John at the Jordan to be baptized by him. John tried to prevent him, saying, "I need to be baptized by you, and yet you are coming to me?" Jesus said to him in reply, "Allow it now, for thus it is fitting for us to fulfill all righteousness." Then he allowed him. After Jesus was baptized, he came up from the water and behold, the heavens were opened [for him], and he saw the Spirit of God descending like a dove [and] coming upon him. 17 And a voice came from the heavens, saying, "This is my beloved Son, with whom I am well pleased." - Matthew 3:13-17

2.   The Self-Manifestation of Our Lord at the wedding of Cana

Lesson: To Jesus through Mary

On the third day there was a wedding in Cana in Galilee, and the mother of Jesus was there. 2 Jesus and his disciples were also invited to the wedding. 3 When the wine ran short, the mother of Jesus said to him, "They have no wine." [And] Jesus said to her, "Woman, how does your concern affect me? My hour has not yet come." His mother said to the servers, "Do whatever he tells you." Now there were six stone water jars there for Jewish ceremonial washings, each holding twenty to thirty gallons. Jesus told them, "Fill the jars with water." So they filled them to the brim. Then he told them, "Draw some out now and take it to the headwaiter." So they took it. And when the headwaiter tasted the water that had become wine, without knowing where it came from (although the servers who had drawn the water knew), the headwaiter called the bridegroom and said to him, "Everyone serves good wine first, and then when people have drunk freely, an inferior one; but you have kept the good wine until now." Jesus did this as the beginning of his signs in Cana in Galilee and so revealed his glory, and his disciples began to believe in him. - John 2:1-11

3.   The Proclamation of the Kingdom of God, with the Call to Conversion

Lessons: Repentance and Trust in God

After John had been arrested, Jesus came to Galilee proclaiming the gospel of God: "This is the time of fulfillment. The kingdom of God is at hand. Repent, and believe in the gospel." - Mark 1:14-15

4.   The Transfiguration

Lessons: Desire for Holiness

While he was praying his face changed in appearance and his clothing became dazzling white. - Luke 9:29

5.   The Institution of the Eucharist

Lessons: Adoration

Then he took the bread, said the blessing, broke it, and gave it to them, saying, "This is my body, which will be given for you; do this in memory of me." 20 And likewise the cup after they had eaten, saying, "This cup is the new covenant in my blood, which will be shed for you." - Luke 22:19-20

References

Handbook for Today's Catholic, copyright © 1994, Liguori Publications

Pray The Rosary Daily, copyright © 1991, Marian Helpers

How to Say the Rosary, copyright © 1991, TAN Books & Publishers, Inc.

The New American Bible for Catholics, copyright © 1970, the Confraternity of Christian Doctrine.

AN ACT OF CONTRITION

O my God, my Redeemer, behold me here at Thy feet. From the bottom of my heart I am sorry for all my sins, because by them I have offended Thee, Who art infinitely good. I will die rather than offend thee again.

FIRST STATION: Jesus is condemned to Death

V. We adore Thee, O Christ, and bless Thee.
R. Because by Thy holy cross Thou hast redeemed the world.

My Jesus, often have I signed The death warrant by my sins; save me by Thy death from that eternal death which I have so often deserved.

Our Father.... Hail Mary.... Glory be....

V.   Jesus Christ Crucified.
R.   Have mercy on Us.
V.   May the souls of the faithful departed, through the mercy of God, Rest in peace.
R.   Amen.

SECOND STATION: Jesus bears His Cross

V.   We adore Thee, O Christ, and bless Thee.
R.   Because by Thy holy cross Thou hast redeemed the world.

My Jesus, Who by Thine own will didst take on Thee the most heavy cross I made for Thee by my sins, oh, make me feel their heavy weight, and weep for them ever while I live.

Our Father.... Hail Mary.... Glory be....

V.   Jesus Christ Crucified.

R.   Have mercy on Us.

V.   May the souls of the faithful departed, through the mercy of God, Rest in peace.

R.   Amen.

THIRD STATION: Jesus falls the First time Beneath the Cross

V.   We adore Thee, O Christ, and bless Thee.

R.   Because by Thy holy cross Thou hast redeemed the world.

My Jesus, the heavy burden of my sins is on Thee, and bears Thee down beneath the cross. I loathe them, I detest them; I call on Thee to pardon them; my Thy grace aid me never more to commit them.

Our Father.... Hail Mary.... Glory be....

V.   Jesus Christ Crucified.

R.   Have mercy on Us.

V.   May the souls of the faithful departed, through the mercy of God, Rest in peace.

R.   Amen.

FOURTH STATION: Jesus Meets His Holy Mother

V.   We adore Thee, O Christ, and bless Thee.

R.   Because by Thy holy cross Thou hast redeemed the world.Jesus most suffering, Mary Mother most sorrowful, if, by my sins, I caused you pain and anguish in the past, by God's assisting grace it shall be so no more; rather be you my love henceforth till death.

Our Father.... Hail Mary.... Glory be....

V.   Jesus Christ Crucified.

R.   Have mercy on Us.

V.   May the souls of the faithful departed, through the mercy of God, Rest in peace.

R.   Amen.

FIFTH STATION: Simon of Cyrene helps Jesus to carry the cross.

V.   We adore Thee, O Christ, and bless Thee.

R.   Because by Thy holy cross, Thou hast redeemed the world.

My Jesus, blest, thrice blest was he who aided Thee to bear the cross.

Blest too shall I be if I aid Thee to bear the cross, by patiently bowing my neck to the crosses Thou shalt send me during life. My Jesus, give me grace to do so

Our Father.... Hail Mary.... Glory be....

V.   Jesus Christ Crucified.

R.   Have mercy on Us.

V.   May the souls of the faithful departed, through the mercy of God, Rest in peace.

R.   Amen.

SIXTH STATION: Jesus and Veronica

V.   We adore Thee, O Christ, and bless Thee.

R.   Because by Thy holy cross, Thou hast redeemed the world.

My tender Jesus, Who didst deign to print Thy sacred face upon the cloth with which Veronica wiped the sweat from off Thy brow, print in my soul deep, I pray Thee, the lasting memory of Thy bitter pains.

Our Father.... Hail Mary.... Glory be....

V.   Jesus Christ Crucified.
R.   Have mercy on Us.
V.   May the souls of the faithful departed, through the mercy of God, Rest in peace. R. Amen.

SEVENTH STATION: Jesus Fall a Second Time

V.   We adore Thee, O Christ, and bless Thee.
R.   Because by Thy holy cross, Thou hast redeemed the world.

My Jesus, often have I sinned and often, by sin, beaten Thee to the ground beneath the cross. Help me to use the efficacious means of grace that I may never fall again.

Our Father.... Hail Mary.... Glory be....

V.   Jesus Christ Crucified.
R.   Have Mercy on Us.
V.   May the souls of the faithful departed, through the mercy of God, Rest in peace.
R.   Amen.

EIGHTH STATION: Jesus comforts the women of Jerusalem

V.   We adore Thee, O Christ, and bless Thee.
R.   Because by Thy holy cross Thou hast redeemed the world.

My Jesus, Who didst comfort the pious women of Jerusalem who wept to see Thee bruised and torn, comfort my soul with Thy tender pity, for in Thy pity lies my trust. May my heart ever answer Thine.

Our Father.... Hail Mary.... Glory be....

V.   Jesus Christ Crucified.

R.   Have Mercy on Us.

V.   May the souls of the faithful departed, through the mercy of God, Rest in peace.

R.   Amen.

NINTH STATION: Jesus falls a third time

V.   We adore Thee, O Christ, and bless Thee.

R.   Because by Thy holy cross Thou hast redeemed the world.

My Jesus, by all the bitter woes Thou didst endure when for the third time the heavy cross bowed Thee to the earth, never, I beseech Thee, let me fall again into sin. Ah, my Jesus, rather let me die than ever offend Thee again.

Our Father.... Hail Mary.... Glory be....

V.   Jesus Christ Crucified.

R.   Have mercy on Us.

V.   May the souls of the faithful departed, through the mercy of God, Rest in Peace.

R.   Amen.

TENTH STATION: Jesus is stripped of His garments and given gall to drink

V.   We adore Thee, O Christ, and bless Thee.

R.   Because by Thy holy cross Thou hast redeemed the world.

My Jesus, stripped of Thy garments and drenched with gall, strip me of love for things of earth, and make me loathe all that savors of the world and sin.

Our Father.... Hail Mary.... Glory be....

V.   Jesus Christ Crucified.

R.   Have mercy on Us.

V.   May the souls of the faithful departed, through the mercy of God, Rest in peace.

R.   Amen.

ELEVENTH STATION: Jesus is nailed to the Cross

V.   We adore Thee, O Christ, and bless Thee.

R.   Because by Thy holy cross Thou hast redeemed the world.

My Jesus, by Thine agony when the cruel nails pierced Thy tender hands and feet and fixed them to the cross, make me crucify my flesh by Christian penance.

Our Father.... Hail Mary.... Glory be....

V.   Jesus Christ Crucified.

R.   Have mercy on Us.

V.   May the souls of the faithful departed, through the mercy of God, Rest in peace.

R.   Amen.

TWELFTH STATION: Jesus Dies

V.   We adore Thee, O Christ, and bless Thee.

R.   Because by Thy holy cross Thou hast redeemed the world.

My Jesus, three hours didst Thou hang in agony, and then die for me; let me die before I sin, and if I live, live for Thy love and faithful service.

Our Father.... Hail Mary.... Glory be....

V.   Jesus Christ Crucified.

R.   Have mercy on Us.

V.   May the souls of the faithful departed, through the mercy of God, Rest in peace.

R.   Amen.

THIRTEENTH STATION: Jesus is taken from the cross and laid in Mary's arms

V.   We adore Thee, O Christ, and bless Thee.

R.   Because by Thy holy cross Thou hast redeemed the world.

O Mary, Mother most sorrowful, the sword of grief pierced thy soul when thou didst see Jesus lying lifeless on thy bosom; obtain for me hatred of sin because sin slew thy Son and wounded thine own heart, and grace to live a Christian life and save my soul.

Our Father.... Hail Mary.... Glory be....

V.   Jesus Christ Crucified.

R.   Have mercy on Us.

V.   May the souls of the faithful departed, through the mercy of God, Rest in peace.

R.   Amen.

FOURTEENTH STATION: Jesus is laid in the tomb

V.   We adore Thee, O Christ, and bless Thee.

R.   Because by Thy holy cross Thou hast redeemed the world.

My Jesus, beside Thy body in the tomb I, too, would lie dead; but if I live, let it be for Thee, so as one day to enjoy with Thee in heaven the fruits of Thy passion and Thy bitter death.

Our Father.... Hail Mary.... Glory be....

V.   Jesus Christ Crucified.

R.   Have mercy on Us.

V.   May the souls of the faithful departed, through the mercy of God, Rest in peace.

R.   Amen.

LET US PRAY

O God, Who by the precious blood of Thine only-begotten Son didst sanctify the standard of the cross; grant we beseech Thee, that we who rejoice in the glory of the same holy cross may feel everywhere the gladness of Thy sovereign protection. Through the same Christ our Lord... Amen ....

PRAYERS SAID IN RELATION TO THE CELEBRATION OF THE HOLY EUCHARIST

PRAYER OF THE CHALICE

A gift of love from the late Bishop Connie Poggiani

O God, to Thee I raise my whole being,
a vessel emptied of self. Accept, Lord,
this my emptiness, and so fill me with
Thyself—Thy Light, Thy Love, Thy
Life—that these Thy precious Gifts
may radiate through me and over-
flow the chalice of my heart into
the hearts of all with whom I
come in contact this day,
revealing unto them
the beauty of
Thy Joy
and
Wholeness
and
the
serenity
of Thy Peace,
which nothing can destroy.

LORD, Father all-powerful, and ever-living God, I thank Thee, for even though I am a sinner, Thy unprofitable servant, not because of my worth, but in the kindness of Thy mercy, Thou hast fed me with the precious Body and Blood of Thy Son, our Lord Jesus Christ.

I pray that this holy communion may not bring me condemnation and punishment but forgiveness and salvation. May it be a of faith and a shield of good will. May it purify me from evil ways and put an end to my evil passions. May it bring me charity and patience, humility and , and growth in power to do good. May it be my strong defense against all my enemies, visible and invisible, and the perfect calming of all my evil impulses, bodily and spiritual. May it unite me more closely to Thee, the one true God and lead me safely through death to everlasting happiness with Thee. And I pray that Thou wiliest lead me, a sinner to the banquet where Thou with Thy Son and Holy Spirit, are true and perfect light, total fulfillment, everlasting joy, gladness without end, and perfect happiness to Thy saints. Grant this through Christ our Lord. AMEN.

AN INVOCATION BY DOM BEDE GRIFFITHS

Eternal light, shining beyond the heaven's radiant sun, illuminating all regions, above, below and across, true light enlightening every one coming into the world, dispel the darkness of our hearts and enlighten us with the splendor of your glory.

A REVISED ACT OF FAITH BASED UPON THAT OF THE LIBERAL CATHOLIC CHURCH

We believe that God is love and power and truth and light; that perfect justice rules the world; that all his children shall one day reach his feet, however far they stray. We hold the fatherhood of God, the fellowship of humankind; we know that we do serve him best when best we serve our fellow human being. So shall his blessing rest upon us † and peace for evermore. Amen.

LIBERAL CATHOLIC "THEE WE ADORE"

"Thee we adore, O hidden splendor, Who in this sacrament does deign to be; We worship you beneath this earthly veil. And thy Presence we devoutly hail."

BENEDICTION (SAID AT THE END OF MASS)

"May Christ our Lord give us the grace to continue our lives in the spirit of this sacrifice, overcoming evil with good, falsehood with truth, and hatred with love. By seeing our good works, may others also come to glorify God. Amen.

In the name of God, the Creator (or Father-Mother), † Word made Flesh, and the Holy Spirit, the Peace of God, which passes all understanding, keep your hearts and minds in Christ Jesus (Phil 4:7).

The Mass is never ended. The Presence is always with us. Let us go in peace to love God and our fellow human beings."

ABOUT THE ASCENSION ORGANIZATION

The Ascension Alliance and Community of Ascensionists is an independent Catholic religious organization and a clerical congregation–among "The Other Catholics." We are part of a spiritual movement and of the Mystical Body of Christ; a Church; an umbrella organization; and an expression of God's mystical movement of Spirit. We draw our lineage, or lines of apostolic succession, from the historic churches, East and West, although we are not a part of the Roman Catholic or Eastern Orthodox communions. We derive our chief western line through the Old Catholic churches of Europe, which separated from the see at Rome beginning in the early 1700s. Our principal Eastern line comes through the ancient churches of India, which are believed to have been established by the Apostle Thomas, beginning in the year 52, C.E., and which were served by Assyrian and Syrian Orthodox bishops for generations. We like to think of ourselves as being born of a "free" Catholic (or universal) vision and a much larger stirring of Spirit, which beckons us to transcend old ways that no longer work, ascend to higher levels of consciousness, and be transformed. In addition, we are dedicated to helping other seekers who wish to do the same.

We Joyfully Celebrate the Sacraments in Communities Worldwide

**Mailing Address:
P.O. Box 167, Vaughn, WA 98394**

Website: ascensionalliance.org

www.ingramcontent.com/pod-product-compliance
Lightning Source LLC
Chambersburg PA
CBHW060725030426
42337CB00017B/3010